OUR AMAZING ANIMAL FRIENDS

A blue whale, largest animal on earth, splashes in the sea.

by Gene S. Stuart

BOOKS FOR YOUNG EXPLORERS
NATIONAL GEOGRAPHIC SOCIETY

Copyright © 1990 National Geographic Society
Library of Congress CIP Data: p. 32

Mammals

Meet some champions of the animal world. Many live on the land. Many swim in the sea. Some fly the farthest. Some run the fastest. A few are amazingly tall, or amazingly small!

Largest Land Mammal

An African elephant is so big that even its baby can be as heavy as a very big man.

Look for the drawings that show you how big some animals are next to a six-year-old child. The last page gives the sizes.

Largest Seal

Largest Primate

With a loud roar, a male elephant seal warns other males to stay away. Adult males weigh more than three small pickup trucks, or 177 first graders.

Gorillas are the largest of all the monkeys and apes, but they are shy, gentle giants. Standing up straight, an adult male gorilla would be as tall as a grown man.

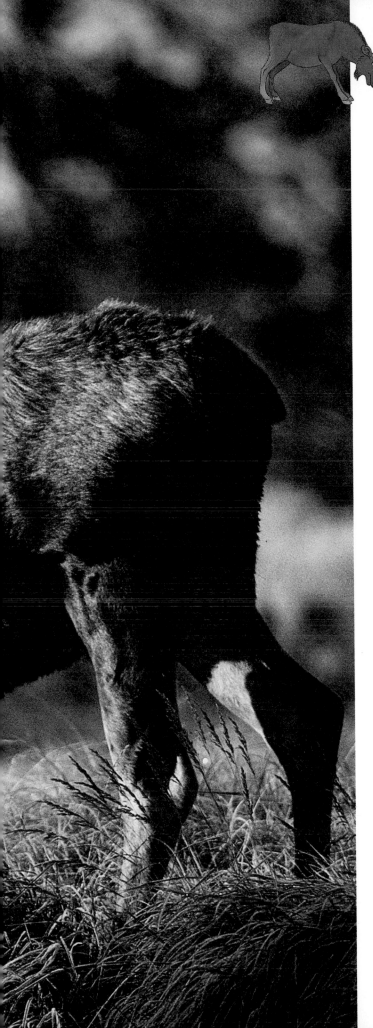

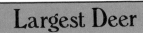
Moose are members of the deer family. Sometimes the males use their antlers to push each other. They are finding out which of them is stronger.

Largest Jackrabbit

Alert for danger, an antelope jackrabbit sits very still. It is not a rabbit at all. It is a hare. This is the largest and fastest kind of jackrabbit in North America.

Largest Cat

A Siberian tiger has grown a thick winter coat that keeps it warm. Tigers are the largest of all cats, and Siberians are the biggest tigers.

Largest Wild Dog

Bending low, a gray wolf stretches in a snowy wood. It looks like a German shepherd dog. Wolves hunt in groups for large animals such as a moose.

Largest Rodent

A capybara cools off by wading. Webbed toes help it swim and dive. Capybaras look somewhat like big guinea pigs.

GROWTH CHART

19
18
17
16
15
14
13
12
11
10
9
8
7
6
5
4

Tallest Mammal

Giraffes are the tallest land animals. You'd be tall, too, if your neck were as long as your legs. A giraffe's neck has only seven bones, the same as yours. Its neck bones are just longer.

Smallest Bear

Expert climbers, Malayan sun bears live in forests. They build nests in trees for napping. Adult sun bears might be about as tall as you are.

Smallest Deer

A pudu is small enough to hide in high grass. This tiny deer belongs to the same family as the moose, but it weighs less than a moose's newborn calf.

Smallest Primate

What's this? It may look like a giant to a little cricket. But this mouse lemur is so small you could hold it in the palm of your hand. These tiny cousins of gorillas eat insects, spiders, small frogs, fruit, and plants.

Fastest Mammal

A cheetah watches. Maybe it is looking for prey. Cheetahs are smaller than tigers, but they are the speediest of all land animals.

Cheetahs have slim bodies and long legs. This shape helps them race after prey. Slowly, silently, a cheetah follows its prey, then suddenly takes off and attacks. For short distances, it can go faster than a car traveling 55 miles an hour.

After a hunt and a big meal, a cheetah likes to rest awhile.

Females with young must hunt often to feed their families.

Fish

Largest Fish

What polka-dot giant looks
like a whale, but is really a fish?
A whale shark—the biggest fish
in the sea! Harmless to people,
the sharks eat small sea animals.

Reptiles

Largest Lizard

Is this a fire-breathing dragon?
No, it's a monitor lizard, also
called a Komodo dragon. It is
more than twice as long as a
six-year-old child lying down.
The lizard uses its forked tongue
to gather smells from the air.

Largest Tortoise

Aldabra tortoises live on islands in the Indian Ocean. A tortoise is a turtle that lives on land. The slow-moving tortoise is famous for living a long time. Some live more than 100 years.

Largest Reptile

A saltwater crocodile is twice as long as the Komodo dragon. It eats fish, reptiles, birds, and other animals.

These reptiles can live on land or in water. The crocodiles can swim in the ocean. They even travel from island to island.

21

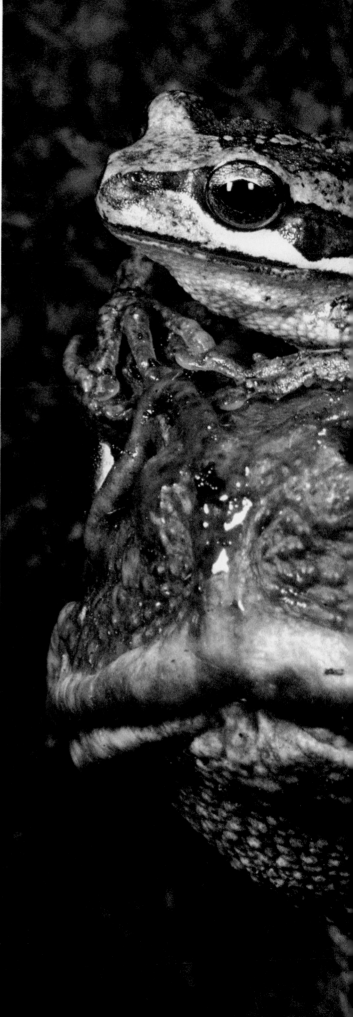

Amphibians

Largest Toad

The striped burrowing frog
sitting on this marine toad's
head would fit in your hand.
A marine toad is dangerous
if an enemy bites it.
Its skin has poison in it.

Frogs and toads are amphibians.
They spend part of their lives
in water and part on land.

22

Crustaceans

Largest Crustacean

This long-legged relative of lobsters and shrimps is a spider crab. It lives in very deep water. Spider crabs take ten years to reach adult size.

Mollusks

Largest Clam

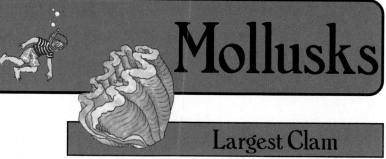

Very carefully, a diver looks at a giant clam. If anything passes over it, the clam closes up. This kind of mollusk has two shells. The animal is inside.

Insects

Largest Wingspan

Long wings make the South American owlet moth an amazing insect. These moths come out at night to feed on flowers. They belong to one of the largest insect families. Butterflies are their cousins.

Longest Butterfly Migration

Millions of monarch butterflies travel a long way, flying across the United States from Canada to Mexico in the autumn. They rest in winter and fly north in spring. These little champs live only one year.

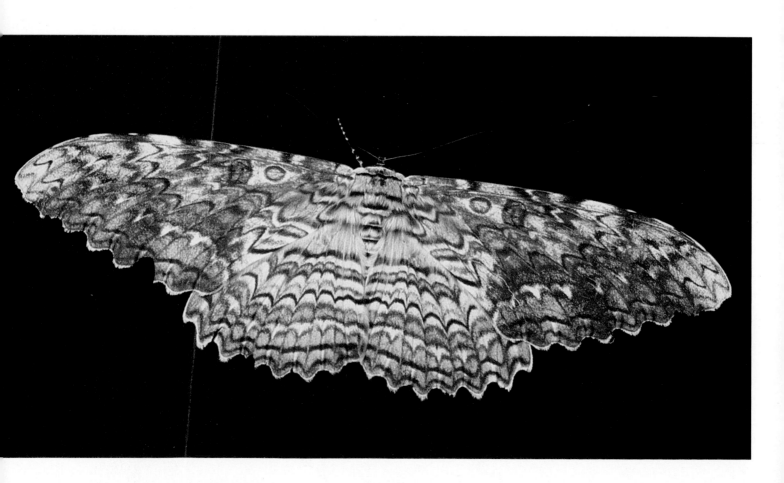

Birds

Largest Bird

Ostriches are birds that do not fly. But they can run as fast as a racehorse, and can keep up the speed for half an hour. They are too tall to enter most doorways.

An ostrich tends its chicks and eggs, the biggest and strongest eggs of any bird living today. One weighs about $3\frac{1}{2}$ pounds.

Longest Bird Migration

Arctic terns migrate farther than any other bird. Twice each year they fly about halfway around the world. In summer, they nest and raise their young in the Arctic. They fly to the coasts of Antarctica for the winter.

A male wandering albatross tries to win a mate by showing off his wings. Long wings help the birds glide easily on ocean winds.

Two giraffes watch for danger. A giraffe is so tall it can pluck leaves from some treetops, with a tongue up to 21 inches long!

COVER: African elephants use their trunks to sniff the wind, to gather food, and to drink. In hot weather, the animals cool off by using their large ears as fans.

Published by

The National Geographic Society, Washington, D.C.
Gilbert M. Grosvenor, *President*
    and Chairman of the Board
Melvin M. Payne, Thomas W. McKnew,
    Chairmen Emeritus
Owen R. Anderson, *Executive Vice President*
Robert L. Breeden, *Senior Vice President,*
    Publications and Educational Media

Prepared by

The Special Publications and School Services Division
Donald J. Crump, *Director*
Philip B. Silcott, *Associate Director*
Bonnie S. Lawrence, *Assistant Director*

Staff for this book

Jane H. Buxton, *Managing Editor*
Dennis R. Dimick, *Illustrations Editor*
Beth Molloy, *Art Director*
Debra A. Antonini, *Researcher*
Roz Schanzer, *Artist*
Sharon Kocsis Berry, *Illustrations Assistant*
Lisa A. LaFuria, Sandra F. Lotterman, Katy Old, Dru McLoud
    Stancampiano, Marilyn Williams, *Staff Assistants*

Engraving, Printing, and Product Manufacture

George V. White, *Director,* and Vincent P. Ryan,
    Manager, Manufacturing and Quality Management
David V. Showers, *Production Manager*
Lewis R. Bassford, *Production Project Manager*

Consultants

Raye N. Germon, National Museum of Natural History,
    Smithsonian Institution; Dr. Thomas A. Jenssen, Virginia
    Polytechnic Institute and State University; Dr. Roy
    McDiarmid, U.S. Fish and Wildlife Service, National Museum
    of Natural History; Dr. Walter E. Sheppard, U.S.D.A.

Agricultural Research Service, Beneficial Insects Laboratory;
Dr. George E. Watson, St. Albans School; William A. Xanten,
Jr., National Zoological Park, Smithsonian Institution,
Scientific Consultants
Susan Altemus, *Educational Consultant*
Dr. Lynda Bush, *Reading Consultant*

Illustrations Credits

Jen & Des Bartlett (cover, 28, 28-29); François Gohier (1); Stephen J. Krasemann/VALAN PHOTOS (2-3); Jen & Des Bartlett/SURVIVAL ANGLIA (4-5); Denis-Huoi/JACANA (5 upper); Jeff Foott (6-7); Thomas Wiewandt (7 right); © Jim Brandenburg (8); Hans Reinhard/BRUCE COLEMAN LTD. (9 upper); Mike Price/BRUCE COLEMAN LTD. (9 lower); David Madison/BRUCE COLEMAN INC. (10-11); Gerry Ellis/ELLIS WILDLIFE COLLECTION (12-13, 14-15, 17 upper); Günter Ziesler/BRUCE COLEMAN LTD. (13 right, 16-17); © Stephen J. Krasemann/DRK PHOTO (16 upper); Flip Nicklin (18-19); © 1990 José Azel/CONTACT PRESS IMAGES (20); Jeff Foott/TOM STACK & ASSOCIATES (21 upper); Steven Kaufman/BRUCE COLEMAN LTD. (21 lower); Otto Rogge/AUSTRALASIAN NATURE TRANSPARENCIES (22-23); Jeff Rotman (24 left); © David Doubilet (24-25); ANIMALS ANIMALS/G. I. Bernard (26); © Jim Brandenburg/DRK PHOTO (27); Peter Hawkey/SURVIVAL ANGLIA (29); Frans Lanting/MINDEN PICTURES (30-31); L. L. Rue III/BRUCE COLEMAN INC. (32)

Library of Congress CIP Data
Stuart, Gene S.
    Our amazing animal friends / by Gene S. Stuart.
        p.   cm. — (Books for young explorers)
    Includes bibliographical references.
    Summary: Introduces record holders of the animal world, including the largest lizard and the fastest mammal.
    ISBN 0-87044-821-8 (regular edition) — ISBN 0-87044-826-9 (library edition)
    1. Animals—Juvenile Literature. [1. Animals.] I. Title. II. Series.
QL49.S825   1990
591—dc20   90-6490
                                                                              CIP
                                                                              AC

More About OUR AMAZING ANIMAL FRIENDS

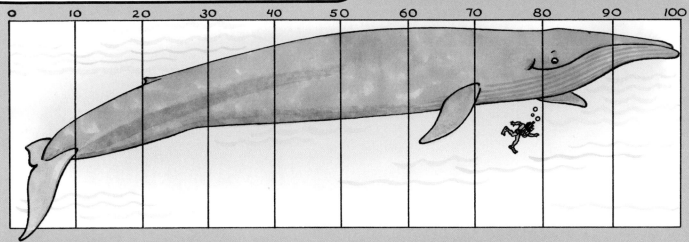

Our six-year-old explorer swims beside a blue whale, the largest animal that has ever lived on earth.

Record holders can be found throughout the animal kingdom. This book shows a small collection of animal champions, from mammals to mollusks.

Imagine the most gigantic animals that have ever lived—massive creatures that began prowling the oceans some 25 to 30 million years ago and still exist today. They are the blue whales (see page 1).

These animals are mammals. The largest are the females, which can measure as long as 100 feet and weigh as much as 176 tons. One can equal the weight of 22 African elephants. At birth, a blue whale weighs about 2 tons. While nursing, a calf may gain 200 pounds a day.

After the young are born, blue whales migrate from warm tropical waters to polar oceans. Except for nursing young, the whales eat little on their migration to frigid waters. At journey's end, they feed

on abundant shrimplike creatures called krill. An adult can eat several tons of krill a day.

The largest living land animal is the African elephant (cover, pages 2-3). Like whales, elephants are mammals. These giants may weigh as much as 8 tons and measure some 13 feet tall at the shoulder. Their massive ears may be as long as 5 feet from top to bottom. A newborn calf stands about 3 feet tall at the shoulder and may weigh more than 200 pounds. Elephants feed mainly on roots, leaves, fruits, shrubs, grasses, and bark. An adult eats more than 300 pounds of food daily.

Another giant, the elephant seal (pages 4-5), gets its common name because of the adult male's trunklike nose. The proboscis may act as a resonating chamber that enables the roar of the bull to carry for miles.

From the largest to the smallest, each kind of animal has a size, a

color, or a shape that helps it survive. But many of the animal champions are endangered. Blue whales were so reduced in number by hunting that only a few thousand remain. African elephants have been killed for their ivory tusks, and fewer than a million are left. Laws now help protect both of these remarkable creatures, and people are working to save them.

Additional Reading

The Amazing Things Animals Do. (Washington, D.C., National Geographic Society, 1989). Ages 8 and up.

The Big Book of Animal Records, by Annette Tison and Talus Taylor. (New York, Grosset & Dunlap, 1985). Ages 7-11.

Incredible Animals A to Z. (Washington, D.C., National Wildlife Federation, 1988). Ages 6-12.

COMPARISON CHART		WEIGHT	HEIGHT	LENGTH	RANGE OR MIGRATORY ROUTE
MAMMALS (cover, pages 1-17, 32, *Our Amazing Animal Friends*)	blue whale	176 tons*		100 feet	all oceans
	African elephant	8 tons	13 feet tall at shoulder		Africa
	southern elephant seal	4 tons		20 feet	coast of southern Argentina, most subantarctic islands, south to edge of Antarctic ice at 78°S
	gorilla	600 pounds	6 feet tall		Africa
	moose	1,819 pounds	7.5 feet tall at shoulder		North America, Europe, and Asia
	antelope jackrabbit	8 pounds		26 inches	Arizona and Mexico
	Siberian tiger	675 pounds		9 feet	southeastern Siberia and Manchuria
	gray wolf	176 pounds		5 feet	North America, Europe, and Asia
	capybara	174 pounds		51 inches	Central and South America
	giraffe	3,968 pounds	19 feet		Africa
	Malayan sun bear	143 pounds		4.5 feet	Southeast Asia
	pudu	22 pounds	16 inches tall at shoulder		South America
	mouse lemur	3 ounces		6 inches	Madagascar
	cheetah	159 pounds		5 feet	Africa and parts of the Middle East
FISH (pages 18-19)	whale shark	20 tons		45 feet	Atlantic, Pacific, and Indian Oceans
REPTILES (pages 20-21)	Komodo dragon	365 pounds		10 feet	islands of Komodo, Rintja, Padar, and part of Flores in the Lesser Sunda Islands
	Aldabra tortoise	560 pounds		4 feet	Seychelles (introduced on some islands)
	saltwater crocodile	1,543 pounds		22 feet	India, Sri Lanka, Andaman and Nicobar Islands, coastal Southeast Asia, Philippines, western Caroline Islands, New Guinea, northern Australia, Solomon Islands, and Vanuatu
AMPHIBIANS (pages 22-23)	marine toad	2 pounds		9 inches	tropical and subtropical regions worldwide (introduced in some locations)
CRUSTACEANS (pages 24-25)	giant spider crab	14 pounds		12-foot claw span	southeastern coast of Japan
MOLLUSKS (page 24)	giant clam	550 pounds		4 feet	southwestern Pacific Ocean
INSECTS (pages 26-27)	South American owlet moth			12-inch wingspan	Central America and parts of South America
	monarch butterfly			3.5-inch wingspan	travels 4,000 miles each year in North America
BIRDS (pages 28-31)	ostrich	330 pounds	9 feet tall		Africa
	arctic tern	4 ounces		15.5 inches	flies more than 12,000 miles twice each year during its migration between polar regions
	wandering albatross	27 pounds		11.5-foot wingspan	southern oceans

*All measurements are maximums.